Grace *Is* Not Just *A* Girl's Name

D1513136

Charlene McCarrell

ISBN 979-8-88943-520-4 (paperback)
ISBN 979-8-88943-521-1 (digital)

Christian Faith Publishing
832 Park Avenue
Meadville, PA 16335
www.christianfaithpublishing.com

Printed in the United States of America

To God, who knew me before I was born and who gave me the ability and strength to write this book. He is with me always.

And to my friends and family who allowed me to share their lives in the pages of my book. Blessings to you!

Contents

Chapter 1

Grace

The year 2021 was a banner year. I felt like I was riding on a roller coaster. My stomach churning, tension around every corner, feeling as if the bottom fell out. My eyesight faded temporarily, my mother died from liver cancer, my retirement, and then my own cancer diagnosis. Part of me was in disbelief. *Come on, God*, I thought. *Really? Where did this all come from?*

Well, although my mom's sickness was surprising, she was and had been down for quite a while. She had congestive heart disease, and her knees were worn out. In a short span of time, everything went wacky. She could no longer do anything on her own and was extremely tired. Her stomach swelled up, and she was having trouble eating. A trip to the hospital told us about the cancer, which I suspect had been around for quite a while, just undiagnosed. My sister Kathy and I were able to share in taking care of the needs of my mom at home due to the fact that I needed to take leave off from work due to my eye problems, which thankfully gave me the time to do this.

Within a week of her being home again, she was gone. Though I was shocked and will always feel an empty spot where she was, I felt in my heart that this was God's mercy stepping in. The day my mother passed, she said to my sister Sharon during a phone call, in a laughing, confident voice, "I am going dancing tonight." And just the night before, while my sister Kim was with her, she also heard Mom speak of dancing specifically with my dad, who had already passed on. She knew and did not doubt. I smile every time I think of

1

this. Her faith in the Lord was unfailing, and you couldn't help but be encouraged by it. God doesn't see death the way we do. Her pain is gone, and she is dancing in heaven!

Looking back at all that happened during this time, I can see the grace of God.

Concerning my cancer, seeing specialists, and undergoing countless tests, I was back on that roller coaster, hanging on with white knuckles and just wanting it to be over! This was a long process, and during it, through prayer and trusting in God, I chose to go ahead with breast surgery and radiation, which I finished a few months prior to writing this. I am taking the hormone medicine now and am undergoing infusions every six months for the osteoporosis they found in my hips, but I am confident the worst is over. I leaned on God a lot during this time, taking comfort in his Word, and hung onto family and friends who were a great comfort to me. And with lots of prayers, I am confident that God was and is in control of all things.

Having Christian faith does not mean I will not have trouble. It is not something magical that takes all your problems away. Jesus actually states in John 16:33 (NIV): "I have told you these things, so that in me you may have peace. In this world you will have trouble. But take heart! I have overcome the world." I am comforted and blessed knowing he has overcome the world, and he is in control.

Author Nancy Leigh DeVoss puts the concept of this subject in a unique way: "True blessing is not the absence of hard things but Christ's presence in the midst of hard places—the grace to dwell with difficulty and still know that He is bestowing upon us the greatest of all blessings: Himself. For that is all we need."[1] A soft whisper of comfort breathed into my heart when I read that and left me with the confidence of the Lord's power at work in me.

I wasn't always like this. It was a long and difficult journey to the truth about God that started the day I was born. This is what I would like to share with you. My journey, my testimony, and how I came to love and trust the Creator of the universe.

---

[1] Nancy Leigh Demoss, "February 15," *Quiet Place: Daily Devotional Readings* (Chicago, Illinois: Moody Press, 2016).

Chapter 2

The Start

You have searched me, Lord, and you know me. You know when
I sit and when I rise; you perceive my thoughts from afar. You
discern my going out and my lying down; you are familiar with
all my ways. Before a word is on my tongue you, Lord, know it
completely. You hem me in behind and before, and you lay your
hand upon me. Such knowledge is too wonderful for me, too
lofty for me to attain. Where can I go from your spirit? Where
can I flee from your presence? If I go up to the heavens, you are
there; if I make my bed in the depths, you are there. If I rise
on the wings of the dawn, if I settle on the far side of the sea,
even there your hand will guide me, your right hand will hold
me fast. If I say, "Surely the darkness will hide me and the light
become night around me," even the darkness will not be dark
to you; the night will shine like the day, for darkness is as light
to you. For you created my inmost being; you knit me together
in my mother's womb. I praise you because I am fearfully and
wonderfully made; your works are wonderful; I know that full well.

—Psalm 139:1–14 NIV

L et's face the facts: I was not a candidate for grace. Yet God was
there from the start of my life and even before that.

I was born and raised in a strict Catholic home with hard-work-
ing parents. My dad worked outside the home, and my mom cared

for us kids inside the home. I was one of *ten children.* They did an awesome job. Rules? Plenty. How else could you have any semblance of order?

My mom was the first one in my life who put a love for God in my being. She planted the seed for God to grow in my heart. She talked a lot about how good and loving God is. It made me feel safe, like being wrapped in a warm embrace. I treasured our talks right up to the time of her passing. She was a strong and faithful woman used by God in a mighty way.

My dad was strict but loving. He did the disciplining, enforcing what we could and could not get away with (which wasn't a lot). He was playful too, though. His mood was often light, and he would tease us, play with us, and let us somersault over his knees while he smoked his pipe and read the newspaper, occasionally reaching a hand out to tickle us. Sometimes, though, it would get crazy, all of us siblings competing for his affections all at the same time. I wonder how he had the patience to deal with that! But he never gave any indication that he was bothered, and we all took advantage of the attention.

All of us siblings had our roles. My two older siblings—Jerry, who was good-looking, popular, and funny; and Kathy, who was always so glamorous to me with blonde, styled hair like a model— were elusive at first. I didn't really know them until I was older, as they were not very involved with us younger ones. They had their lives and places to be.

The next two brothers, Michael and Brian, dedicated their lives to making our lives miserable, driving me crazy with their tickling and teasing. One time, sitting in the backyard with my best friend, Jenny, one of my brothers sat down and said something corny like, "When Charlene showers, she needs to run around under the showerhead to get wet and not fall down the drain," (a tease about being skinny). Then, "The other day, Charlene put her bra on backward, and it fit." Once he got a laugh from my best friend, which he always did, the jokes revved up. You would think he had a book of skinny jokes hidden away; he had so many. It often ended up with me in tears, feeling small and rejected, and hating the fact that I was so skinny.

The pain I felt more than the jokes being shoveled out was my best friend's response. Yes, I hated being skinny due to the fact it made me an easy mark, but the laughing of my so-called friend, I felt, was a betrayal of everything friendship was supposed to be. In my mind, she was supposed to be defending me against my brother, not siding with him. I could feel a part of me closing up during that time of my life, an insecurity that pointed out there was something about me that didn't deserve that type of friendship.

Looking back, that was the beginning of many lessons that ended up making me a vessel for the Lord. You see, regardless of my shape, I was fearfully and wonderfully made, as the psalm states above; I just didn't realize it yet.

That psalm shows me now how my heavenly Father knows me intimately. He orchestrated me in my mother's womb. Reading that further on in my life was like a light revealing God's love for me and for all of us. All that to say, don't be too hard on Michael and Brian. All brothers are pains in the neck. Although one of those brothers has passed away, the other is now a strong Christian man who means so much to me.

The next sibling in the line-up is my sister Sharon. She is the outspoken and protective mothering type, for me anyway. She graciously let me put my arm around her when the fears of the night would reach in and grab me, and helped a gawky, shy, sixth-grade girl transform into a beautiful princess for my first dance. She put rollers in my hair and brought it up on my head with dangling ringlets. My mom made my dress, and although I can't exactly remember what it looked like, I know it was beautiful because I felt beautiful! Yes, Sharon was a comfort to me. That left me to mother the last four.

Carol was the sister immediately younger than me. She was quiet and smart, a typical tomboy, and though I would never admit it to my best friend, was so much fun to play with! Patty was strong-willed and said whatever was on her mind, whether it was good or bad. She loved training and riding horses. Her active life was cut off at an early age when she came down with Multiple sclerosis at sixteen and slowly deteriorated up to her death at thirty. The blessing to this story is that although, for many years, she nursed a bitterness for this disease that ravished her body and dug a hole in her heart filled with anger, during her last years, she embraced God and got so much comfort from this group of kids that would visit her at the nursing home. She found peace at last, which was so evident the last time I visited her. It was shortly after that when God took her home.

God's Word states in 2 Peter 3:9 (NIV): "The Lord is not slow in keeping his promise, as some understand slowness. Instead he is patient with you, not wanting anyone to perish, but everyone to come to repentance." Sometimes it is true that the Lord may take us through darkness, but always remember, joy comes in the morning (Psalm 30:5). It is God's promise. The thing is, he is not willing for any of us to be lost and will do whatever it takes to bring us into life. Patty once told me that she was glad for her MS. She confessed if she had gone on the way she was going, she would have been lost forever.

The Lord patiently waits for us to embrace his free gift of salvation, which Patty finally did. At her funeral, a favorite verse of hers was read from John 14:2–3, where Jesus says, "My Father's house has many rooms; if that were not so, would I have told you that I am going there to prepare a place for you? And if I go and prepare a place for you, I will come back and take you to be with me that you also may be where I am" (John 14:2–3). That is where she is now, in her prepared place, healed and free from pain. God's grace is abundant.

Bill was the child who came after Patty. He was gifted with a huge heart and has this unique sense of humor that leaves us all laughing even now. We had a rule in our house that shoes needed to be taken off at the door for everyone *except* those wearing dresses. Bill decided to test this rule. You see where I'm going with this! He walked down in one of Kim's dresses with his shoes on. I don't even think dad could object; we were all laughing so hard. By the way, Bill, you look pretty in pink!

Lastly there was Kim, the baby of the family, who was spoiled by all her older siblings! She has a good heart and a bold wit, which may shock you or crack you up laughing depending on the moment. That's what makes her so much fun to be around. My mom entrusted me to these last four, which was fun at times and a pain at others, like when I was hanging out with my friends. I was not always the best sister. There were times like when we would play hide and seek, but Jenny and I would take off. I did love them, and there were many times when we all played together, always having fun!

So that was my family. Not too different and blessed with great parents. Alas, the shaping of my life had started, and life continued on in its journey.

I let life circumstances shape me, and instead of reacting in love and forgiveness, I chose to let fear rule my life. I bought into the lies. I was this skinny, clumsy child that did not matter, scared of my own shadow and willing to be anything for anyone to get approval yet unable to express myself, which made me self-conscious and shy. I simply did not know at the time how to stand up to these lies and instead let them consume my life with shame and loathing.

Chapter 3

Jenny

My best friend was a very troubled girl I will call Jenny, though I did not know she was struggling at the time. Her parents were the best friends of my mom and dad. She was two years younger than me, but somehow, we were the ones that became friends. She was reckless and wild, demanding loyalty. When she did not get what she wanted, you could expect a spoon shoved down your throat and quite possibly a choking, whichever object was closest. She was needy and craved control.

But to me, she was exciting and fun, confident and brave, and I put blinders on to the real dangers in this friendship. I was her puppy and wanted to do what she did, think like she did—basically be just like her. No matter how hard I tried to be the best friend I could, I failed. She would always let me get so far, then she would crush me, pointing out my faults. And she could find a lot. One time, she told me and my sisters to sing the "Twelve Days of Christmas" in front of my family's Christmas gathering, then proceeded to laugh and tell us how awful we sounded, even though the family and company clapped. Another time, I trusted her with some of my writings to see if they were good, and again laughing, she tore down each one. I was so impressionable at the time and believed everything she said. Each time she came back at me throughout the years, it just added to my belief that I was not worthy of friendship. It hurt to the core that I was just not good enough.

As I got older, I realized just how human Jenny was, and my awe and admiration for her faded, replaced with sadness and compassion. I saw how she never seemed to be happy no matter the endeavors she took on. Although she never confided in me, it was obvious that there was something within her that was keeping her from any joy in life.

We cannot begin to know what causes some people to act the way they do. When I was young, I had no idea what friendship or relationships meant. I was grateful for any attention and did whatever was needed to make it work. It was one-sided for both of us. We both wanted something without giving back that, in the end, resulted in neither of us getting what we needed. It left us both hurt and broken. Many years later I learned the true meaning of friendship through learning about the love of God, that he loved us so much that he gave his only son as a sacrifice for our sins. This is how we are to love others. Putting away our needs freely and giving of ourselves without wanting something in return.

Chapter 4

School

S omeone extremely near and dear to me told me she did not believe in God and the Bible was written by old men who hated women. I found this incredibly sad, as I believe the Bible is a love story and actually showed honor to women in several verses, including the story of the woman brought before Jesus for the act of adultery (see John 8:1–11).

At first, I was bound and determined to prove to her that Christ's love was written in every line. I went and dug up verses that showed his love for us, then thought again about the why. Why would she believe this? Could it be that when statements like these are made, there are some other underlying emotions involved, maybe anger or hurt, regarding life experiences they have dealt with or are dealing with in their lives now? Maybe someone who has hurt them using Bible verses out of context for control or manipulation? Maybe they have not actually sat down and read the Bible. Maybe they are not aware of the depths of God's love.

In truth, there are deceivers out there that masquerade as people of God and do horrible things in God's name. None of us are perfect, and it is by the grace of God that he works in us to create new beings. It's our choice to accept or reject this grace. We are given the choice to use it for good or, as some have done, for manipulation and evil. Wanting to use this for good, I questioned, "How do we break down the lies and deceit of the enemy and show the truth?" I did not, as my dear brother has said, want to be standing on the highway, handing out water bottles to those on the way to destruction. Pondering this brought me back to my beginning days of school and how the lessons of life continued.

My parents placed us in a Catholic school that had so many rules my poor little mind couldn't comprehend them. Nuns in their inky black habits and always-stern faces, hardened by life, believed that to really serve God, you needed to deprive yourself of any of this world's pleasures, as that would take you away from God. They believed the more you suffered, the closer you were to God, which sadly meant suppressing all joy and grace in their lives. I find it strange considering that the heart of God is love, which brings joy and grace.

The school was sparse, nothing bright and cheery. Just the teacher's desk and our desks and chairs in each classroom. All other rooms were the same. Nothing inviting or comforting in view. It was daunting, and I felt small and insignificant being there. I was shell-shocked for the first year, hardly opening my mouth unless I was asked a question. It was no wonder I flunked that year. It was all so hard for me to take in, I was confused most of the time, and there were no kind words to help me through. Learning came hard, and keeping the rules were your only means of survival, which weren't posted anywhere. You learned as you went along, usually the hard way.

We all had separate lunchrooms and playgrounds (boys/girls, and no playground equipment); rules to follow before you went out to play (getting into line and keeping quiet); and rules before you came back in from recess (the first time the principal rang her bell meant for you to freeze; after she walked around, making sure there was no movement in the playground, she rang the bell a second time and we got into line again, quietly, and went back in our rooms). You had to raise your hand to speak, even for going to the bathroom. Oh, but do not raise your hand during a test, whatever you do! This exact rule resulted in my first public humiliation.

There I was in the second year of first grade, sitting at my desk, having to go to the bathroom, not being able to concentrate on the test, and trying so hard to hold it in. I did try to raise my hand but was met with the cold glare of the nun. After what seemed like hours (probably only minutes), I watched in horror at seeing that stream

11

run down under the desk in front of me. The shame and humiliation pounded in my head, unable to move, just wishing no one would see. The only thing I can remember is being sent home and that awful sinking feeling of shame. From then on, it went downward.

Years of abuse at the hands of the nuns, harsh words, sardonic teasing, singled out in class for everything done wrong, and comments such as "Sit up in your chair, Charlene, before you slip through the crack."

Another time in fourth grade, I flunked a math exam. Because I had been out sick so much, I never grasped what was being taught. My teacher gave me a child's counting bar with big red beads on it and made me use it whenever we were doing math problems. Feeling shame over and over again, I was so anxious and nervous during those years, knowing that I would never measure up, never smart enough to learn. The more I tried, the more I failed. I thought if I was quiet enough, they would ignore me, but strangely enough, it only made it worse. It was like I had a bullseye on my forehead that said, "Here I am!" It seemed I was always getting pulled up to the front, starting with the words, "See, this girl here, she…"

How did this affect my popularity, you may ask? I had one main friend in school (Jenny went to public school.) I will call her Sue. Her parents were friends of my mom and dad, just like Jenny's parents. It was pretty much expected that we would be friends. She was like Jenny, though, bold and controlling. She had other friends who followed her around, doing her bidding. Although I did not crave to be like her, I pretty much did whatever she told me to do out of fear. You did not want to be on her bad side.

One time, she was mad at me for some reason I can't remember (but I am sure it had to do with her being jealous of Jenny or some other girl I paid attention to), and she formed a line with her other friends, hand in hand, her being at the end. We called it a snake, where the leader would start a fairly fast run across the playground then, all of a sudden, take a sharp turn, which would throw everybody to a sharp right. I don't know how she did it, but as she was thrown to the right, it was always at the precise place I was playing, she lifted her hand up right across my face. *Oops!* Of course, it was always an accident.

Another time, not an accident, she pulled out a handful of my hair in the bathroom of the school then threw it back at me. That time, someone I was with grabbed it and told the principal against my wishes. I just wanted to slink away, unnoticed, and pretend it didn't happen. These assaults were frightening and confusing to me, leaving me shocked and torn up, not understanding what friendship was and why friends would act like this. Feelings of hurt and shame always followed, always feeling at fault for it all.

The principal called me and her into the office, and Sue knew she couldn't lie her way out of this one because you could see my roots in the hair follicles. It couldn't be explained away as an accident. Sue told me beforehand that we better make up or else it would not end well for me. I kept my mouth shut and only nodded to her story. I let her do the talking, which ended up with her in tears because I had become friends with another girl and would not let her into their friendship. She was hurt, and this was why she pulled my hair. She understood that this was wrong but just wanted to be my friend. I was shocked but did not speak, quietly wanting it to be over and just be out of the office.

In the end we had to apologize to each other—her because of what she did, and me for making her feel bad for hanging out with someone besides her. It ended with a forced hug. Everything was "good" then. We were friends again, and my attention turned back on her out of fear and nothing else. Strangely enough, I never mentioned these instances to my mom and dad, as I knew they were friends with Sue's parents, and I did not want to make it worse. I felt so alone, having no one I could confide in. Jenny would most certainly turn it back on me, and there was no one else I trusted with my feelings. I just kept telling myself it wasn't important. It didn't matter. *I* didn't matter, which again is what the school taught me. I continued to follow the rules and believe them as truth:

1. Do what is expected of you. Your worth is in how you measure up.

2. Keep your head down and go along with whatever is presented to you. Do not make waves in anything, and trust no one!

I can now see how the conclusion that there is no God and that "the Bible was written by old men who hated women" may be the belief of some people.

Somehow, I intertwined God in this equation. At the time, although never reading the Bible myself (only listening to those who taught it), there was no place for me in God's world, as I was so far from being perfect. The words taught mocked me. How could God love me when I was such an utter disappointment? Self-pity seemed to swallow me up during those years, leaving me stuck in bondage and unable to move forward. Any anger I felt was tucked safely inside me. After all, the Catholic school also taught that anger was a sin, so that is where I believed it belonged.

Now I know that all that is so far from the truth!

Writing this leaves me with a question: How can you tell someone about the truth of love, something that goes beyond your looks and how you see yourself?

My friend, the world tells us we are not fearfully and wonderfully made. We are not lovable, smart enough, too shy, too short, too tall, too fat, too skinny, too ugly, have a big nose, have bad teeth—the list goes on and on. Those are lies. I did not know it then, but think about it. God's Word tells us over and over of his love for us. We have a choice to believe his Word or believe the lie and continue to live in self-pity, stuck in our own despair.

What if we looked into the mirror and said, "I am not perfect. But I am loved by God, who will never forsake me, and that is enough"? I don't know about you, but when I first realized that, it brought a sigh of relief to me. I finally felt I didn't need to waste any more time trying to be perfect. I was loved just as I was. Roman 8:38–39 (NIV) is just one of the many verses that state this: "For I am convinced that neither death nor life, neither angels nor demons, neither the present nor the future, nor any powers, neither height nor depth, nor anything else in all creation, will be able to separate us from the love of God, that is in Christ Jesus our Lord" (Romans 8:38–39 NIV).

How I wish I had learned that when I was a child.

Despite all that happened in the Catholic school, those years didn't make me bitter toward God. I doubted he could love me, but that did not stop me from loving him. My thought then was that I just needed to earn his love—do better and be better.

Chapter 5

Moving On

We moved away during the academic year in sixth grade, but I had frightening dreams about that school for years. It wasn't until I was in my thirties and walked down the halls that I realized it was just a building that couldn't harm me. I no longer needed to hold on to the fear that school put in me, and I am grateful for that.

The move itself was painless. My parents helped us to adjust to the new house and make everything welcome. I was actually excited to move. I did not have any friends or circumstances to miss and was hoping for a new life. Unfortunately, although I had moved away from Jenny and Sue, they were not out of my life because of the friendships between my parents and theirs. We would visit back and forth in the summer at different times, but their control in my life was still there; and I still felt the same as I always had: unworthy and destined to be a failure. A shadow that was always over me.

One thing that did change is that I went only to public schools from that time on. That was another world in my mind, and again, I felt shell-shocked for the first six or seven months. I went from a totally controlled environment to extreme chaos. Unruly kids talking out loud in class, often over each other, no hand-raising, and no discipline. We could eat with boys and play with boys, and there were no rules in the playground. No rules for going to the bathrooms. I should have been ecstatic, but the utter chaos made me nauseous; and I often felt sick to my stomach, unable to make sense of what was going on. I fell behind in my studies and did not feel calm for quite a while. I did manage to make a few friends, however; and after a while, I started to get used to that school, although I never felt comfortable talking out in class.

Chapter 6

Taking Another Step Off the Cliff

In seventh grade, I stayed overnight at another friend's house. I will call her Jane. She seemed normal enough, although I really had no notion of what normal was. She invited me over, and I said yes. She was my age, fourteen, and was somewhat of a tomboy, always playing rough at school—mostly sports. During my visit, she attacked me sexually. She was strong and forceful, and I was no match for her. As I was crawling away on my hands and knees in terror, trying to get away, she overpowered me.

My parents had protected us from the world. We were not even allowed to leave the block we lived on unless they gave us permission to do so. They monitored what we watched on TV, and we knew little of this world and the evils in it. The fear and shame I felt was to such a degree that I felt frantic. All I knew was spinning out of control during this unbelievably horrible scene. I believe I started crying and screaming, and her parents came in. Jane said we were just goofing around, and I was speechless. Nothing came out of my mouth. I was literally frozen in my fear.

She laughed it off and left me alone the rest of the night, but I spent the night with this new fear inside me again, unable to move and not really understanding just what had happened. This incident left me feeling so devastated and dirty that, out of desperation, I did tell Jenny, hoping for some kind of understanding and comfort; but she only laughed and thought it was so funny. I was truly stricken. Again, her words hurt me beyond what I could deal with.

The next time I visited her she put one of her friends up to making a pass at me. It was horrifying. I believe it was during this time that I lost my voice. I never spoke to anyone about myself or my emotions. I shut up and put up with everything in silence, hoping that the silence would make whatever happened go away and burying it deep down inside myself. Later on, I wondered why I didn't tell my parents about this. I think I just felt ashamed and felt it was not worth the fuss. My mom was not the cuddly type, but I knew she loved me. This was just too ugly, and I did not feel safe talking about it. I didn't feel comfortable being alone in a room with another woman outside my family until my late twenties.

There began to grow an anger down deep within me, hidden from the world and even from me most of the time. It would come up in force when silly things would happen, like dropping my comb or when my hair was acting up. Hairpin triggers that were short and lasted only seconds. I could not explore these feelings because, as I said before, anger was a sin. I sank low, and my life's ambition from then on was to find someone to love me for me. What I didn't know was that I could not love until I forgave, and I couldn't forgive because every emotion and incident was crammed so deep inside of me, willing itself to be forgotten.

One of the things I took joy in was drinking, which started around fourteen. It gave me back my voice. I was able to be something I wasn't able to in normal day-to-day life—bold! That is what I chose to believe anyway. The first time, it was at a party my older brother and sister had at my mom and dad's house while they were away one weekend. My brother's friends kept slipping me drinks until I was wasted! I loved it, and they thought it was funny; but I felt a power I never felt before. I could talk to people, say whatever I wanted, and for a while, be the center of attention. That was my new source of confidence. I could forget the real me for a while, and that was what I wanted.

My mom and dad never knew any of the things I was doing. I didn't talk to them during this time about anything going on in my life. It wasn't that I hated them or anything. Like most teens, I figured they were parents. What do they know? There was a part of me that felt guilty for deceiving them, and part of me did want to be a good girl that they could look up to; but I knew I wasn't, so I didn't try. I kept their rules and tiptoed around the rest. God was trying to break through at different times, but I squished him down and chose to ignore his quiet prompting. How long would it take me before I listened to him?

My life continued to spiral downward from there. I drank and tried some drugs, but not heavy ones. I still needed some control. One night when I was seventeen, I was at a party of one of my friends and was drinking hard. It finally got to the point where they put me to bed to sleep it off. While I was there, a friend of my friend came in and took advantage of me. Thanks to the grace of God, I do not remember much of it, though it affected me greatly. I fell into depression, wondering what was wrong with me that someone would do that. For a while, I had hoped I was pregnant, to have someone to love and have someone to love me. But, thankfully, it was not God's will.

Time went on, and I continued down the road of self-destruction. Drinking led to promiscuity. I suffered one more attack, this time when I invited a seemingly nice man to dinner. I went into that same fear mode, frozen and unable to move or say anything while being used in such a vile way. I still could not get to outward anger at that time and again turned the anger inside, hating myself for being so weak and so unlovable. One more mark against me was my thought at that time.

All three experiences were shrugged off as just bad memories to throw out and move on. The thing is, I never got on with it. Every time I dated and my date made a pass, I felt powerless to stop it. The only exception being when I was completely drunk and could be bolder. All I wanted was love and affection, someone to tell me I was worth something. I had this twisted idea of what was right and wrong that left me with one alternative. The only way I could ever make it right with God and achieve the love I wanted was to get married.

Most of the men just dumped me after the sexual part was over, which left me with more feelings of guilt and shame, but the two times I married were results of me trying to make it right with God and seeking love. I talked myself into believing I loved them, and they loved me; although I had no idea what love was. Both times there were warnings before I got married that they were not the type of men I needed to be with, words spoken that were not kind, and emotions that were confusing and did not add up to love. I, of course, ignored the warnings.

As I will explain later, both marriages were mistakes, although there was a time in the first where I had hoped it would work out. I knew nothing of what a marriage relationship meant. I just thought it was being submissive and doing what was expected of me, ever quietly. In the first marriage, it cost me the relationship between me and my daughter, which has now been restored, thankfully; but her hurts, I feel, may still haunt her. The second marriage cost me my relationship with God, which has now also been restored but with a cost.

You see, while God can bring good from the wrong paths we take in life, they will always cost us, as sin does. Though the world has painted God as this controlling, uncaring entity that restricts us with rules and regulations, this could not be further from the truth. Yes, we have the commandments, and the Bible teaches us to live a moral life; but we need to see that this is for our good, to save us from the hurt and despair that comes from breaking these commandments. The lies I chose to believe, the way I lived my life at this time and, in turn, caused pain to others was the cause of my despair; and getting married was and did not make my life right in any way, neither with myself nor God. There were costs to these decisions, plain and simple.

If I can bring you any comfort in all this, it would be that both you and I can rejoice that there is indeed a way out of this pit we put ourselves in—someone who will hold us and comfort us in good times and bad, not judging us for the mistakes we make. I learned this when I finally gave my life to the Lord, and he forgave my sins right then and there. I knew that I could not erase the past, and there would be a cost; but after time, he did repair my relationships, as is his promise per Isaiah 61:7 (NIV), which says, "Instead of your shame you will receive a double portion, and instead of disgrace you will inherit a double portion in your land, and everlasting joy will be yours."

From the depths of my heart, I can say this is true; and when I finally learned this, I no longer felt controlled or restricted. I felt loved and cared for. I was and am still free to make decisions about my life; I just choose to make them according to Scripture. To choose life over death.

Chapter 7

A Strange Turn

When I was twenty-one, I was getting worn down by depression and bad habits to the point that there seemed to be no purpose in life. Nothing had changed inside me, and I wanted something different. I wanted my life to mean something. Of course, the reasonable way to go about this would be to turn to God, but I still believed I was in charge of my life and was depending on myself even though I had no idea how to go about changing my circumstances. At that time, I only felt this loneliness in me that never stopped hurting, and I just wanted it to stop.

Where was God during this part of my life? Believe it or not, he was there, softly calling me, just waiting for me to call on him. There was still that seed in me that wanted to grow despite my actions, and still, at times, I could feel it there, trying to take root. Unfortunately, my mind would start moving again, and rebellion would win in the end.

In my desperate, futile, continuing quest for love and acceptance, I ended up pregnant. Of course, the guy did not want anything to do with me or my pregnancy. He had already fallen in love with another woman, and I hadn't seen him since the weekend I became pregnant. I had mixed feelings about my situation. Part of me was happy to be pregnant, and my heart soared at the thought of having someone to love and to love me in return. The other part of me felt dread; the knowledge that I was not married, which was a sin; and the fear of how my family would react to the news, being a strong Catholic family!

The first three months of pregnancy left me so sick I could not take care of myself; my mother came and took care of me. That was when they heard the news. They were not happy, but being in control of their emotions, as they always were, there were no loud angry voices. It was decided, quite calmly, that I would give the child up for adoption then go to college and start my life again with a solid education and career. That was it: situation avoided, and no more discussion needed.

That worked for the first six months or so, but I always felt conflicted about this plan. I started having dreams about my baby being born and there being a feast set in front of me. Everyone was celebrating; but then I would see my mom's stern face staring at me, and I would feel deflated, knowing the celebration was in error. I finally confronted the fact that there was a huge need inside me to please my mom. I could not both keep my baby and please my mom.

Due to the fact that I strongly feared facing her with my emotions, I wrote her a letter explaining how I felt inside and how I could not bear to give this child of mine up for adoption. I added that I already loved her and wanted her in my life. I told my mom about the dreams I was having and hated to make her unhappy but felt I could not go through with the adoption.

Her response was surprising. She said that she sensed I was in turmoil over this and suspected I would have a problem giving my baby up. She went on to say that she trusted that the Lord would take care of me and told me to do what was in my heart! I cried when I read that letter, so relieved that she understood. Her words also helped me to have a better understanding of unconditional love. That ended my conflicted dreams, and I felt content and confident that she was right when she said that God would take care of us.

I believe now that Jesus who, as I mentioned earlier, uses all things for good, used this pregnancy to bring me back from the brink of destruction. My thoughts at this time were not wondering where the next party was or how to get a guy. It was on keeping myself and my baby healthy.

It was a hard, emotional pregnancy and birth. I had to have a C-section because my baby was breeched, but the moment I saw my beautiful daughter, Ruth, I fell in love. It was a love I had never felt before. Love not grown out of need, but a love that swallows you up and consumes you. She was perfect in my eyes. My family also loved her instantly and doted over her. She was definitely a wanted and loved child!

As she grew, we had our challenges and hardships. I relied on government support until she was two, then went to work for minimum wage. I had no work skills, so there was not much out there. I still had food stamps, but with daycare, it was very hard. My mom's words were true though: the Lord always provided for us. We never went without, which is quite surprising to me now because I still hadn't turned my life over to God. I did start going to church again, but I still knew nothing about relationship with God. He loved me and Ruth regardless of this, which I know now is there in his Word for all to see, and it fills my heart with joy.

Ruth was a beautiful child, as sweet as any person could be, but had a stubborn side just like her mother. This gave a new meaning to the terrible twos! When she went into one of her tantrums (luckily, it was not often), you'd better batten down the hatches and prepare for a storm. Thankfully, they did not last long, and when she was finished, she was so sorry for what she had done. She knew even then it was not right to act that way. She always had such a good heart.

I was certainly not equipped to be a mother and had made vast mistakes, so you can probably understand when I say we grew up together.

Chapter 8

Marriage

One vast mistake I made was when my daughter was ten. I met a man—I will call him Jeff—and decided to marry him for all the wrong reasons. I was so tired of forging on my own, and he seemed so nice and caring at first. I felt a lot of compassion for him. He had emotional baggage that was heartbreaking.

He came from a broken home where his mother married a man that often abused her physically and the kids emotionally. Jeff was filled with a lot of guilt because he could not protect his mother from the beatings and, in turn, was hurt by his mother because she did not protect him and left this abusive man. When he asked her why later on in life, she said, "He was exciting."

Being the youngest of three, his two older siblings—being old enough to take care of themselves—were gone as much as possible, and he was left alone to cope with this. He tried twice to go outside the home for help. One time, he called the police, who came, but they spoke with his stepfather outside, laughing and joking while his mother lay bleeding inside. He never told me what happened when his stepfather came back in the house, but I can imagine it was not pleasant. The other time, he talked with a teacher at school, who told him there was nothing she could do, as they don't get involved with problems at home. That was the way in the '50s.

His mother finally left her husband and married a wonderful man when Jeff was around fourteen. He was the only good father Jeff had ever known and loved the kids a lot. All too soon though, there was tension, and his mother left this good man and went back to her first husband. When Jeff asked why, she said, "He was not exciting enough." At that time, he was sixteen and refused to go back into that abusive situation, so he asked his mom to let him enroll in the army. She agreed and signed the form. The army may have removed him from the abusive home, but it did not heal the scars that ran so deep inside him.

I was Jeff's third wife. The first marriage resulted because of a pregnancy and ended right after his son was born. The second lasted sixteen years as a constant battle, including affairs from both and a mixture of extreme hurt to each other followed by making up and doing something drastic to save their marriage—whether it be buying a new place to live in or getting involved in some new project.

I came in after his wife at that time had walked out on him with a new love interest. He boldly told me he wanted to protect me and my daughter, and I was more than willing to give him that job. I know now where that was coming from, but in reality, how could he protect us when he was so badly broken himself?

Those first few years were a nightmare. Anything we did or did not do brought fury to him. He raged and broke dishes or whatever was near, yelling so loud and hard his face would redden like a tomato and he would visibly shake. I was always paralyzed with fear, my mouth glued shut. I did not have the ability to protect myself or my daughter.

Actually, that is not true. I always had the ability; I just did not have the strength to stand up to this anger in front of me.

I hated myself for that and felt so much guilt for being weak. I didn't get angry at Jeff for any of the times he acted out. Once again, the anger went inside myself. I knew that I should have done something, but I also thought the anger was safe there and wouldn't harm anyone around me. But it did harm. It harmed our relationship, keeping it stunted; and more so, it harmed my beautiful daughter and her tender heart.

I remember thinking we were lucky because there was never any physical abuse, but I didn't realize emotional abuse was just as bad. Ruth must have felt as alone as I felt, and Jeff too, each of us in our little private wars. I was constantly tiptoeing around the house and was encouraging my daughter to do the same, thinking if only we do this or that, he would calm down and not be so angry. Healthy relationships are not structured around preventing anger. And it never worked for long, and our home remained a battle zone.

During that time, we started going to church. One of my husband's friends I met would tell us about Jesus, acting like they were best friends, and say he talked to Jesus and that Jesus actually told him that his wife who had left him was coming back in October (something that actually happened in October, two years after I had met him).

Well, of course, I thought the guy had lost a marble or two. I mean, come on. Jesus talked to him? But after a while and many questions later, I really wanted that peace and confidence he had; it seemed so real. We decided to try his church out and were amazed at the message from the Bible that showed a loving, caring God that I had only heard about from my mother in years past. We were anxious to learn more about this God, so different from the God taught to me in the Catholic school. They taught, from the Word of God, of a salvation that did not come from works—not something to be earned, like I had thought my entire life, but a gift freely given through his son Jesus Christ, who willingly sacrificed his life for us by dying on a cross.

The Bible also talks about a love so sweet and pure, like Lamentations 3:22–23 (NIV) says, "The steadfast love of the Lord never ceases; his mercies never come to an end; they are new every morning; great is your faithfulness."

We both wanted this gift and the grace of God. We received this free gift by first hearing and understanding the message, believing and proclaiming Jesus is Lord, repenting of our sins and rebellion then being buried with Christ in Baptism, and being resurrected to a new life in Christ (see Acts 2:22–41 and Romans 6:1–7). That day was my first public declaration of a life I wanted with all my heart and will never forget the joy of that conviction. I know now that Jesus will never force us to make this decision. In his love, he has given us free will. This must be a personal decision.

Per Revelation 3:20 (NIV), he says: "Here I am! I stand at the door and knock. If anyone hears my voice and opens the door, I will come in and eat with that person, and they with me." He states that he is knocking, but he will not intrude. Is this a God who is controlling and unloving, as the world tells us? I say no! It was his gentle nudging that caused me to look and decide, and I tell you that the blessings I have received are beyond anything you or I could imagine.

Chapter 9

A New Life

I would like to state here that living a life for Christ does not come naturally. Like everything else in life, it is learned. Unfortunately, some of us are slower than others.

Although we had dedicated our lives to God, our home life was still in turmoil. The rages had not ceased; they became unbearable. It seems we had dedicated our lives to the Lord but separately. Instead of working as a team to grow in the Lord, we did everything we thought we were supposed to do as Christians—go to church, read the Bible, stop partying, stop listening to secular music, etc.—but continued to live our personal lives the same way we always had. We still didn't understand the relational part of knowing God and the need to surrender our lives to him. We still thought we were in control of our lives.

It got to the point where I could see no other solution than to leave my husband. We separated, and my husband found a group run by a pastor of a small church near us. He was hopeful that he could get the help he needed. We both started attending the meetings and church there, though at separate services and meeting times. This group was run by an ex-con who had been saved in prison and then became a pastor. His testimony was powerful and touched both of us deeply. He started this group to help those who needed to know the saving love of Christ. There was an interesting mix of people with all kinds of problems, but all wanted healing in their lives. We fit right in.

With time, we did change. Through the grace of our Lord Jesus Christ, we started learning about relationship and the depths of his love. Through God's gentle voice guiding us, we got back together and went through counseling. Jeff truly had changed, and we were committed to making this work; but through all the turmoil, we just did not understand that the damage done to my daughter could not be undone as easily. She only went to counseling a few times, but when the counselor made references to my husband changing, that was it for her. She had a hard time trusting. How hard it must have been for her!

I did not know how to handle this. Trusting others was an issue I had fought with my entire life. How could I teach someone else to trust when I had still not resolved this issue for myself?

That was the beginning of the end. The more my husband tried to reach out to her, the more she resisted, angry and rebellious. The tighter we held on, the angrier she got. Finally, she started running away. I felt like I had failed, and the pain in my heart was unbearable. Still though, we turned to others instead of God. Had we learned nothing?

Not knowing what to do, in desperation, we joined a tough love group and clung tight to that. I am thinking now that it was a way to get control back in our hands. That old familiar lie that if we are in control, everything would be okay. But it was not okay. I had no more control in what was happening around us than I did when I was a child. I did have God now and the assurance he gave me that this would turn out well. I loved my daughter as much as my heart was able to and thought tough love would make her see reason. All it did was turn her away and put my daughter through two years of drugs and trying to survive on her own. She was only fifteen at the time.

I called every authority during those years and was told time after time there was nothing anyone could do for me. Even the police finally told me to let her go. The only way I could keep somewhat of an eye on her was to talk to the assistant principal at the high school she was going to at the time. He would talk with her once in a while and would tell me how she was doing and reassure me she was all right. That was until she dropped out of school. It was then that a government representative told me I had the right to take her to court, and if I could prove she was unsafe, they would step in and help her. It turned out well, and soon after, she moved in with the grandparents of a friend of hers. I was thankful for some stability in her life, and we began slowly to mend our relationship.

My daughter is an amazing woman. She was not your typical runaway. Although she did quit school in her senior year, she kept a job throughout this whole ordeal. How many runaways would do that? She went on to get her GED. Then after working in the banking world a few years, she wanted to do something that brought a sense of purpose to her life, and she put herself through nursing school. It was not easy, but she stuck with it and is now a compassionate and caring registered nurse.

She has this unique ability to see things not normally seen by most of us, which started when she was young. One time when she was only seven or eight, she saw a child who was handicapped on the bus and noticed that no one was paying her any attention. She got up and sat by her, keeping her company. Per Ruth's words, "She looked so sad." I have heard so many nursing stories from her where she has had this kind of unspoken compassion. It's not something she purposely brings up; you can see it between the lines. She has a strong and caring spirit, and I love her so much! She is someone I will always look up to and admire.

I got my family back; but the prince of darkness was not through with us yet, and we were still blind.

A few years later, a failed church brought disillusion to my husband. He was devastated by it, and as a result, we began searching for a new church. My husband was clearly disheartened by the last church, and no matter what church we went to, it never lasted for long. I could sense a change in him, subtle at first, but he was growing away from God.

Our lives began to crumble. The more he was denying his feelings and moving away from our anchor, the Lord, the more helpless I felt in trying to help him. He was removing the solid rock of Christ that held him up. An opportunity came up then for him to buy some land, a cul-de-sac, and build houses—something he was good at doing. He talked his son from his first marriage into being partner and borrowed the needed money from the bank. Disaster followed.

As the expenses kept coming in, my husband opened several credit cards and maxed them out. Every house that sold, the payment went back to the bank because of what we owed, yet my husband kept hoping it would work out. He kept all this from me, and since he took care of the business aspect of our marriage, I did not see the bills that kept building up for us. We ended up in bankruptcy. We tried to remortgage the house, finishing it up to sell, but that fell through because our house was built around a trailer that no banks would finance. It resulted in a much lower sale than the house and five acres were worth, the entire payment going to the bank for costs we owed.

In the end, my husband, sober for fifteen years, started drinking again. That's when I felt sure I had lost him. He started staying out for weekends, then all holidays, then even a couple nights a week with his brother and friends. He could not even look at me and turned away if I tried to touch him. I saw him maybe three times a week, and even then, he was not truly there. I was a reminder of a life he did not want anymore. Even in his sleep, if I accidently brushed against him, he would kick me away. The tears I cried were immeasurable, so sad to see what had become of our marriage and helpless to stop what was happening.

I must be honest at this point. Did I do all that I could? The answer again was no! Stuck in self-pity, and still blind to the truth. Instead of turning to God in prayer, I pulled into myself, just wanting to be alone. Church did not relieve the heartache I felt, and I refused to reach out to my family for support. I certainly did not reach out to my husband and talk to him about what was happening. Instead of being a helpmate in this time of distress, I let him do as he pleased and even blamed him for the ruin of our marriage.

It was my dear daughter who told me I needed to confront him and ask if he wanted to save our marriage. Fear rose up in me at first. I was not the type of person to confront anyone, scared of what he would say. I asked myself: was it safer to be quiet, silently hoping he would come to his senses? I knew then I would have to be the one to say something, hoping he would say he wanted this to work. But he did not say yes. He said, without emotion, "No, I do not want to save our marriage." I found out later there was another woman he had let into his life.

Strangely enough, that sparked a hope for the first time in a long while. Maybe it was just that I finally knew where his heart lay, and my uncertainty as to what would happen had finally been decided for me—something I was still unable to do on my own. I moved out, got an apartment, and got divorced. I was still going to church and was quite hopeful for the future.

Family surrounded me during that time, showing their love and concern for me, and again I leaned on them for comfort. Still though, I kept them at arm's length, as I still had the notion that I was responsible for myself. I had not changed. Although my knowledge in the Lord had grown, I still had not surrendered myself. I still had not grasped that he was in charge of my life. I was going through the motions while keeping my eye on the world. Well, we all know how that goes!

Chapter 10

Second Time Around

Then I met whom I thought was the love of my life. He was a man whose smile could light up the room, a man full of confidence and a man whom everyone looked up to. Was he a believer? No, but he did not mind if I was one. I told myself I would go into this relationship on my terms; I would demand an equal relationship. He encouraged me to do things I had never been able to do because of fear, and in turn, I felt fearless!

Oh boy! Like I mentioned before, there were warning signs upfront. He could not tolerate weaknesses in people and was blunt and somewhat cruel whenever I showed mine. In return, I ignored this and tried all the harder to be strong and stand up to him and my fears. We moved to Eastern Washington, away from my family and closer to his, and we married. Ruth was an adult by this time, having been on her own for several years, and therefore did not move with us.

Joseph was a schoolteacher, probably the best feature about him. He primarily dealt with special needs but not always handicapped. The special needs were mostly learning disabilities. He had a heart for this and truly made a difference in the kids he taught. They loved and respected him. The way he taught with discipline mixed with honesty and care, he actually gave the kids the desire to learn, at least in the beginning. As the years went on, his hands were more and more tied by the rules of the school on what and how he could teach. The school system removed conventional discipline from the classroom and went with their belief that school is for fun, and learning will result from that. Without the ability to direct the kids with the discipline needed toward learning, the classroom became unmanageable, though he still gave it his best.

We brought out the best in each other but also the worst. I depended on him like breathing and did everything in my power to please him. Was it what he needed? No, it was not. It worked for the first couple of years, then it seemed the more compliant I became to him, the more he wanted and needed. I did not have the strength to be everything he wanted, and it discouraged him, which in turn made me feel like a failure again and not worthy to be loved. He could be cruel and uncaring, and it would cut me to the bone. Instead of opening my mouth and standing up to him, time and time again I retreated silently and tried all the harder to be what he wanted. Nothing had changed really. I was still back to walking on eggshells, trying to earn his love. My heart would ache, waiting for a smile from him. As time passed on, the smiles were fewer and fewer.

One night, out of nowhere, he announced that we had reached a point in our relationship where intimacy was no longer needed, that we had outgrown the physical needs of a marriage. I remember looking up, thinking he was joking or something, but he looked serious and even happy at the realization he just had. Although I did not agree, I didn't know how to react to that, and so the conversation ended. Although I was not aware at the time, but this was the start of his letting go.

As time went on, he was getting more discouraged and disappointed with life, talking about suicide and just wanting to die. Although he had always suffered from depression, it was deeper now than I had ever seen before. He hated life and all it stood for. He often said he hoped he would not wake up the next day. This scared me beyond reason, but whenever I talked to him about it, he would just get mad and say, "I am not going to do anything." But one thing he did do was to let go of me.

He hardly acknowledged me unless it was in disappointment or disdain. If I talked, he would just ignore me and say nothing. I hated to call him on the phone because he would be angry, like I was bothering him. He slipped away, bit by bit, and I was heartbroken for him and me. I felt helpless not knowing how to help this man I loved. I entered a dark period myself, depressed and hurt, helpless and hopeless. I tried counseling at my church. The gal was great, and she gave me tools on how to cope with his moods; but it did not fix our marriage or my husband's depression and despondency. There were times I ached for a simple touch, a kind word. His indifference cut me to the bone.

One last incident happened before the end came. I was out working in the front yard and had borrowed his truck to transfer the yard debris to the backfield. I had started early so I could have his truck cleaned up before he left for his class reunion. While working in the yard, my back completely went out. I went back in the house and laid down, thinking it would ease up in a bit. When my husband came in, I told him I could not finish the yardwork due to my back, and he stormed out of the front door. I didn't see him for a while, and when he came back in, he said I was not to work in the front yard anymore. I had gotten some rocks mixed in the brush, and they got caught up in his shredder.

I said I was sorry, but it was too late. It was always too late. During the next three days, I crawled on my knees to the bathroom and kitchen, pulling myself up using the table and chair to eat and take care of myself. I asked him once to help but was only met with anger and disdain at my helplessness, actually saying in disgust, "Yes, you are helpless." It was then that I gave up. I told him I was leaving, that I could not take it anymore. He tried once to stop me, saying he didn't want me to leave. There was so much of me that wanted to cave in, that wanted to try again, but there was also something inside of me that knew it would not work. The anger and hurt I felt over and over again had completely broken me. I knew I just could not do it. With a heaviness in my heart, I realized that the depth of his depression was like a blanket wrapped tightly around him. There was just no room for anything else in his life. I knew I had to go.

Driving away was one of the hardest things I had ever done. A part of me still loved him, and the thought that I had let him down gnawed at me. Also, the knowledge of still another failed marriage left me empty and heartsick. It was not an easy decision to make, but I knew in my heart that the Lord was with me, and I took comfort in that.

Now that time has passed, I do feel that it was the right decision. We enabled each other, gave each other excuses for our behavior. In the end we harmed each other more than helped each other.

Chapter 11

Starting Over Again

I moved in with my mother and my sister, who was also staying with my mother due to a failed marriage. The comfort I received from these two women was just what my heart needed to rest on. Their faith in the Lord strengthened me, and my walk with the Lord continued to grow strong.

A few months later, my sister bought the house across the driveway from my mom, who owned it, and I moved in with her. I also had the blessed opportunity to develop a closer relationship with my daughter, Ruth, now that she lived closer. She is truly the best part of me. Along with all that, I was able to keep my job with Wenatchee Valley Hospital working in the insurance denial resolution department which offered me the ability to work from home, which was such a huge blessing. Thanks be to God.

No… Looking back, I was not a candidate for grace.

And yet it has been given to me over and over again.

During the last year of my marriage, when I was near rock bottom, I noticed a church on my way home from work. I'd driven this route home for years now and had never noticed it even though I later discovered it'd been there for five years!

I went to that church the next Sunday, visibly shaking like a leaf. I was sure that I had burned my bridges with the Lord and wandered up to the front desk. There, a beautiful godly woman must have seen my shaking hands and reached out with the simple gesture of just placing her hand over mine. I felt the Spirit breathe into me, and *whoosh*, I immediately relaxed. She invited me to sit by her, for which I was grateful. The group came on stage, led by a man full of more energy than I was feeling. He started playing the guitar and singing with the rest of the group.

They were incredible. The music swept through my body, and the words of worship felt like rain coming down on me, refreshing my spirit. I felt a love in my heart that I had not felt for so long. The same man with the guitar turned out to be the pastor. As he spoke the message, I knew then that the Lord was still there with me. I felt a belonging in my soul that I wanted to grab and never let go of. Toward the end, however, when he mentioned this was an evangelical covenant church, my first instinct was to run! There was no way anyone was ever going to get me to evangelize. Sorry but no! I was the type of person that came to church, heard the message, then slipped out the door before talking to anyone. I did not have the time or the energy for anything else!

Praise God. He knew better, and after a few weeks of nudging, I was back in church. I could tell right away this pastor had a heart for God. He was funny but no-nonsense when it came to the Word of God and not apologetic. He was true to Scripture, presenting it like a love letter wrapped around humor, common sense, grace, and love. The love of Christ shone through him. I was beginning to feel the stirrings of God's love anew in my heart.

Oh, yeah… God was using this man to show me and others the truth. Was this man of God perfect? Heck no! He was a man, like everyone else in which he freely admitted, but he allowed the Holy Spirit, the giver of life, to work through him and to grow him into this messenger of life, giving good news to the lost.

I began to see God as my God and his teachings as one who wants the best for me. I felt no more condemnation when I read the Bible—only the knowledge that it was written for me to help me learn to grow and written in love to show me a new way to live. It was the first time I realized believing in God was not a spectator sport; that in receiving his love, it was meant for giving back out to love those around us.

Yes, grace is free through the sacrifice of Jesus on the cross, given as a gift to all of us who ask. But I learned that once you receive this new life, you are left with the knowledge that grace does not sit on the couch. It grows as you grow, and the more you let his grace in, the more your heart fills with the love and longing to share it with others.

I listened and took notes on the pastor's messages and read the Bible. I joined home groups and a class the pastor was teaching on leadership. The first step of faith that God chose for me was when the pastor asked us to greet those near us. Normally in churches, I would stand and not move. If someone shook my hand, I would shake theirs, and that was that. Now I stood up and shook the hands of those near me. Then I walked out into the aisles and greeted people in God's power, not mine. What a blessing that was to put a smile on people's faces, make newcomers feel as comfortable as the way I was treated.

The next step of faith he chose for me was to volunteer to be a greeter, like the wonderful gal who greeted me when I first came to the church. That was a little harder for me. I tend to be on the shy side and not particularly good with words, but God reminded me, not by my power but by his. So there I was, greeting people, and God's grace pulled me through. Soon after, I was looking forward to the days I was called to do this.

Wow, Lord. What next?

From there, the assistant pastor said she was going to start a prayer ministry different from the ones currently done in the church and asked me if I would be interested in helping. This would take place on Sunday during communion. While the rest of the team stood up front, we would be in the back standing by two chairs so people could sit down and talk if they wanted to. Was I interested in praying with people? Me, the woman who couldn't think of the right words when I prayed by myself! She told me to pray on it, and I did.

While I was out walking one morning a few days later, the Lord put in my heart these words for me:

I may not be a leader, but Christ Jesus can lead through me.

I may not be eloquent with speech, but Christ Jesus can speak through me.
I may not be able to reach out to people on my own, but Christ Jesus can reach out through me.

Then he showed me,
All I have gone through has been for the glory of God.

All my pain has brought me closer to God and shown me that it is only through him who gives me strength that I can be free to do these things.

It reminded me of his limitless love for us all. It is his perfect love that drives out fear (1 John 4:18). If I lead, comfort, strengthen, love, and reach out to others, it is through Christ Jesus I do these things. Oh yes, I joined the prayer group, and who knew that I would be blessed a thousandfold for just stepping out in God's grace? For in praying with others, I felt strengthened also. In sharing their concerns, it filled me with compassion and the desire to see the Lord glorified in their lives.

One Sunday, my pastor asked the congregation if there were a few of us that would be willing to stand up before the church and tell our testimony a couple of weeks from then. I did not think about it right then, but as the week went on, I kept feeling an urging in my soul telling me I needed to do this. This was the biggest stretch yet: to stand in front of the whole congregation and tell them about my past. How, Lord? Not in my power, but in my Savior's power. I told my pastor I would be willing to share my testimony.

Although a much shorter version than this book, the writing of it was painful. I must have rewritten it at least five times, each time as painful as the first. I finished it, and stepping out in faith again, I stood before the congregation and told my story. When the service was over, I was amazed at the people who came up and gave me a hug, telling me how they were affected and related to my testimony. God once again had given me grace and started my healing.

In writing this book, God has been with me, not only show-ing me the abuse, rejection, struggles, and pain I experienced at the hands of others but also at times opening my eyes to the trials and pain of others around me. He showed me that the people in my life also may have endured abuse, rejection, struggles, and pain. Then he showed me the people he put in my life to show me his truth and grace. However hardheaded and stubborn I was—starting with my mom at that early age and the knowledge that all I went through was for a purpose, ever teaching me—he prepared me for what he intended for me to do. Opening my heart to be able to love those around me, to understand their pain. It was his love, his mercy, and his grace that helped me to understand how easy it is to give up and let sin into the depths of our souls, often unaware of what it is that we carry—always wanting something more and never satisfied with what we have.

Then most of all, he showed me that he has been by my side always, even when I ignored him and turned away. He still loved me, and he always will. He held me up when I didn't have the strength to go on. He never gave up on me, and my dearest, *he will never give up on you either.*

This brought me to a new area of healing in my life. One that would help me to let go of the past and live forever in his love.

Chapter 12

The Grace of Forgiveness

Although I may not have had control over what others have done and said to me in my life, I did (and do) have control over how I choose to react to any abuses done to me. And through prayer, I have come to realize how much forgiveness transforms from a noun to a verb. A concept to an action. It takes effort and steps forward.

For God gave us all free will, and the way we choose to use this gift is our own decision. Each one of us is accountable to God and God alone for our choices in our life, which leaves me as the sole person responsible for myself and my actions alone.

I knew I could not do this alone and asked the Holy Spirit to guide me. I felt a feeling of relief and comfort when I realized I would not be going through this alone.

Chapter 13

Taking Baby Steps

You may be asking yourself now, "How can I forgive someone who has hurt me so badly and through the world's eye does not deserve forgiveness?"

Indeed! This took me to the Bible, and the answer I got was actually a question: "How could I not forgive those who sinned against me!"

The bitter truth that I found is that I am a sinner and have made choices in my life that hurt those around me. Instead of leaning on the strength of God, I chose to live in fear, cowering to those around me and allowing their sins against me to take root instead of standing up and correcting in love, which I know now I should have done. Instead of protecting those given to me, I was the one who said nothing and let the abuse continue. Yes, there was fear, but if I had put my trust in God, he would have removed it as he has now done. For this, I lived in misery and dragged the ones around me down into that same misery and hurt. It was my choice to react the way I did. It was I who needed to ask for forgiveness.

And yet, for all time, there was God who loved me before I was born. He knew the days of my life, what I would do, and how I would react; and yet he still loved me and has been pursuing me my whole life not with condemnation but with love. The condemnation that I felt was a self-imposed lie from the devil. God loved me (us) enough that he gave his one and only Son, Jesus, as a sacrifice for me (us) and my (our) sins (John 3:16).

He was born of a virgin, was ridiculed throughout his whole life, but chose to reach out to those wanting to know of the salvation he spoke of, forgiving and healing all those who asked. Then, at the end, he was betrayed by one of his own followers, with—of all things, a kiss—and then turned over to the earthly authorities to be tortured and condemned to death on a cross, nails put into his hands and feet hung up to die. And what sin did he commit to deserve this kind of death? What awful thing did he do? *He loved us!* The Jewish leaders were jealous that he called himself a King, which is exactly what he is.

Dearest one, he went willingly to the cross, taking our sins upon him so that we might be freed from sin. How humbling this makes me feel that he would do this for me! Tears are in my eyes as I write this. His words on the cross speak of his heart, "Father, Father, forgive them, for they do not know what they are doing" (Luke 23:34 NIV).

If Jesus, who was sinless, died for me and forgave me for all I have done, again I ask, how can I not forgive those who have wronged me?

Chapter 14

Declaration

I willingly forgive, of my own free will, all who have wronged me and forfeit my right to hold a grudge against them. I release them from any wrongdoing and pray for their salvation in the name of Christ, my Savior. And to those whom I have hurt throughout the years, I am so sorry! You did not deserve to be treated that way. I pray for your healing and hope that one day you can embrace the light of the world in Jesus Christ.

Again, this was not easy, but I feel the healing touch of God in my life. A freedom from the chains that held me down for so long. I have a lightness in my step that was never there before, something I wish for all those suffering from pain in the past.

My walk is different now. I still struggle at times with unwanted emotions, but I know now how to quiet my mind, meditate on my Lord, ask him to intervene for me, and pray for him to be my strength. None of us will ever be perfect, not until he comes back for us, but I am happy living with my sister Carol, whose burst-out-laughing sense of humor and yet disciplined manner keeps me grounded. We have a lot of fun together.

I have found a loving Scripture-grounded church and am surrounded by my loving family who is always there for me. Especially my daughter, Ruth, whom I am so grateful for and who is in my heart. I also have Christ-believing friends that I study with, and we support each other as we learn more about our loving God.

As far as having a man in my life, I am happy to be by myself because I am not alone *ever*! My Lord is with me, my constant friend and Savior! I do not need to prove to anyone my worthiness, my importance, because he knows, and that is enough.

Where exactly am I at today in regard to my testimony, and what am I learning and have learned?

I have learned that life seldom turns out the way you plan it to be. Although you may have times of peace where everything goes smoothly and perfectly, that is not the norm. In our crazy upside-down world, life happens. An unexpected diagnosis, the death of a loved one. A tragic accident. Circumstances that take us away from going to college or getting the dream job that will make our lives secure. Spouses or friends that turn out to be less than you expected. Who knows what it is for you. Along with this I have learned, when these things happen, it is not the end of the world. Maybe none of this was ever intended for you in the first place. Maybe there is something better, beyond what you can imagine.

I laugh when I think of myself in the scope of all this. I mean, I never intended to have the friends I did, go to a school that thrived on humiliation, have a baby out of wedlock, have two failed marriages, have cancer, and have eye problems. Pretty crazy, huh? What I have now, though, is so much more. Although I am still struggling with the cancer drug side effects and how tired and achy they make me, these things are happening to my body, but they are not me. This is life!

I am not afraid of what life can do to my body with the fact that one day I am going to die. We all are. Just like my mom, I know where I am going, and there is no fear in that. My confidence is in the Lord. He keeps me grounded as I daily get into his word in the Bible, enjoy the Bible studies I am in, and love and cherish those around me. I live in an imperfect world that seeks to put fear in my life, telling me what I can and cannot do while also saying I am in control of my destiny. Why in the world would I even want to go there?

I have learned what becomes of being in control of my destiny, and it never brought me happiness. The Lord is my driver now, and my goal is to get to know him deeper and to do as he does, to love and be there for those in need. To give of myself as he gave to me for as long as I am in this earthly body. I am learning more every day, and although I may stumble here and there, I can always get back up again and push on!

I praise my God for giving this to me. You may think you are not a candidate for grace, but my friend, never underestimate the power of our Lord, Jesus Christ!

References

Demoss, Nancy L. 2016. "February 15" in *Quiet Place: Daily Devotional Readings*. Chicago: Moody Press.

About the Author

Charlene McCarrell—retired at sixty-seven from a career in medical billing—was inspired to write down her testimony in the hopes of reaching out to others in need of healing and restoration in their lives.

She resides in the Pacific Northwest, spending time with her adult daughter and "grand-doggie," her large family, and her dear friends.

Printed in the USA
CPSIA information can be obtained
at www.ICGtesting.com
JSHW081136210823
46845JS00001B/83